Ref

0825

...tell them, "The Beatles Are Your Salvation!"

by

Diann Venita Bobbitt James

authorHOUSE™

1663 LIBERTY DRIVE, SUITE 200
BLOOMINGTON, INDIANA 47403
(800) 839-8640
WWW.AUTHORHOUSE.COM

First published by AuthorHouse 02/07/05

ISBN: 1-4208-1517-2 (sc)
ISBN: 1-4208-1518-0 (dj)

Library of Congress Control Number: 2004099222

Printed in the United States of America
Bloomington, Indiana

This book is printed on acid-free paper.

IN LOVING MEMORY OF
MY BELOVED DAUGHTER,
ALLISON DENISE HUNTER SMILEY

Table of Contents

Introduction ix

Chapter 1 When It Rains, It Pours 1

Chapter 2 The Dream 13

Chapter 3 "She (He) Loves You" 19

Chapter 4 "Get Back" 27

Chapter 5 "Yesterday" 33

Chapter 6 "I'm a Loser" 39

Chapter 7 "Help!" 45

Chapter 8 "Hey Jude" 53

Chapter 9 "Act Naturally" 57

Chapter 10 "Eleanor Rigby" 65

Chapter 11 "Nowhere Man" 69

Chapter 12 "Ticket to Ride" 75

Chapter 13 "Every Little Thing" 81

Chapter 14 "Devil in Her Heart" 85

Chapter 15 "All You Need Is Love" 89

Introduction

"The Beatles Are Your Salvation" is a divinely inspired writing, and maybe this is my divine purpose. However, I must admit that I wrestled with the idea of doing something so avant-garde, and especially involving religion since I am not a Theologian.

The inspiration for this writing came following a very harrowing experience in my life, and at the time I know that I was very much in tune (excuse the pun) with God. I listened very intently to what he placed on my heart and in my reasoning to communicate to the world. As you read this writing you will also know that this is a special message.

The lyrics of the Beatles' songs are primarily about love relationships between men and women. I had the challenge of writing a book that refers to these lyrics and then writing life lessons in the context of the teachings of Jesus Christ and the love relationship between God and man.

My inspiration to write this book came after the untimely death of my youngest daughter, Allison. I dedicate this writing in memory of her.

Allison Denise was a fun and loving child who grew into being a beautiful wife and mother. All she ever wanted was for people to live in peace and to love one another as God has asked all of us to do — "Imagine." Perhaps her seemingly untimely passing at the age of thirty (30) put me in a higher dimension, and/or maybe God just simply chose me (an ordinary woman) to carry a very special message to the world.

There are many people who assume that an individual has to live a pious life to do the Lord's bidding in a big way. Let me tell you that that kind of thinking is passé and wrong. In the Bible (the word of God) there are many testimonies of instances where he chooses the ordinary person to do extraordinary things. Not only do we read about figures like Joseph, Moses, and David, but down throughout the ages, simple folks have been chosen to fulfill God's divine purpose.

John Lennon once said that the Beatles were bigger than Jesus Christ. He now knows that they were not. But I believe that even as John uttered those words, God was making plans to use the Beatles to reach millions in a way that neither they nor I ever expected. Every living soul has the opportunity by the grace of God through our Lord and Savior Jesus the Christ to be accepted into the Kingdom of God. I surrendered all. What about you?

Chapter 1
When It Rains, It Pours

Every little gust of wind was a chilling reminder...

*F*ollowing the tragedy of the World Trade Center on September 11, 2001, the nation was in a deep depression of spirit. There was a doleful atmosphere everywhere for weeks, to say the least. Americans, in particular, just could not shake it off; even the folks who were not necessarily patriotic. I guess we were all waiting for the infamous "other shoe" to drop. It was sort of like that song "American Pie" —"The day the music died". (For some reason, I never cared too much for that song.)

One evening shortly after the terrorists' attacks, I was driving home from my office, hoping to avoid the remnants of a tornado that the weathercasters reported as having been spotted in Northern Virginia, just south of Washington, D.C. Since I was traveling on the opposite side of D.C. in the state of Maryland, I thought there was little chance of my being caught up in it. Unfortunately, I still had to travel home through a very violent thunderstorm.

As I approached the crossroads of the local Interstate and a local state route in Maryland that went through the township of College Park, I said out loud, "Lord which way should I go?" Accidents are a common occurrence during rush hour in the Washington, D.C., metropolitan area, and especially, whenever it rains. Anyway, I could have sworn that the Lord told me to take Route 212, so, straight ahead I proceeded on Route 212 in my Grand Cherokee Jeep.

As I drove along, I noticed high in the sky a very ominous looking black cloud moving in pretty fast and filling the sky so menacingly. It got my attention because it wasn't the normal dark gray storm cloud. It was kind of billowy like smoke. But, before I could think much about the cloud's black color, the wind started blowing up furiously, and the trees were bowing down to the ground under the force of the tremendous wind pressure. I even had difficulty steering straight.

Driving slower now, I continued to forge ahead still pondering the strange, foul weather, when directly in front of me I saw the leaves and branches of a giant Sycamore tree suddenly open up like a flower and blow away leaving only the skeletal remains of the tree trunk behind. The sight was riveting. That giant tree was made to look like one of those little blow weeds that grow in summer. (I'm talking about the white fuzzy things that dandelions turn into, that pepper grassy fields, and kids pluck up and blow.)

At that very moment, I could clearly see that the black cloud that I was looking at from afar now went from the sky all the way down to the ground. It was a huge tornado. I had never seen anything like that before in my life! I gasped for air. My heart started to race rapidly. This awesome and massive cloud came barreling down on me like a locomotive. But, how could this be? There was no warning on the news or weather!

The vehicle in front of mine turned-around a corner, and I turned right behind it. The street that we turned onto looked to be a dead-end street with small hills or high ground on either side. I saw the driver of the other car (my guardian angel) duck down in his car, and I followed suit in mine, but the console between the seats of the Jeep was in the way. There was no time to get out and to get under anything. Then looking up through the window I realized that I had stopped beneath trees that were sure to fall under the great force of the wind. At that point, my heart was beating so hard I thought it was going to come out of my chest.

From the position that I was lying in, I could only see the rooftops of houses and the treetops twisting in the wind, so I lifted up my head and peeked through the front window to see what else I could see. Just as I raised my eyes over the dashboard I saw a metal guardrail at the end of the dead-end street being ripped from its place. Under the great force of the wind this heavy metal object seemed to float along like a little girls hair ribbon blowing in the breeze, only, it came flying straight at me with the force and speed of a wrecking ball. I ducked down, covered my eyes, and braced for the impact and flying glass, but instead of smashing into the front window, the piece of metal flew over the hood of the Jeep.

The entire time that I was stopped, the wind had been doggedly trying to lift the Jeep off of its tires to take it, God knows where, but for some reason it could not. I naively attributed that to the fact that I was nestled between two little hills on both sides of the street, and that the wind could not get the lift it needed. Just as that thought ran through my mind, looking up I saw a huge tree falling down on the driver's side of the jeep. There I sat strapped in, leaned over, helpless, and waiting to die. There was no time to unbuckle my seatbelt and scramble to the rear. (As though I could have done so in those few seconds.)

I grasped the gold cross hanging around my neck, and called on the Lord Jesus Christ. While lying in a crooked fetal position, I started rocking and saying over and over again, Lord Jesus please be with me.

The tree crashed hard, only it fell short of the jeep, with just the tree top branches hitting the window. Then just like dried up tumbleweed, the tree was lifted up by the wind and it blew away. By now the sound and fury of the wind was simply terrifying. It sounded like a thousand roaring lions. The Jeep was rocking on its wheels very violently, but I held on tightly to my cross and I kept calling on the name of Jesus, over and over again, asking Him to please be with me.

In my helpless state, I knew I was done for, but I did not care if I died; I just wanted the Lord Jesus Christ there with me. Normally, on a daily basis I would talk with my husband and my oldest daughter throughout the day, but on that particular day, I had not. As I laid there preparing for certain death, I thought about the fact that I would not have the chance to say good-bye and or to tell them that I loved them. I remember feeling sad, but then I noticed that the wind started to die down. As quickly as the tornado came up, it ended, and I was still alive. I started to cry uncontrollably.

I could not see out of my driver's side window and barely out of the back window, because they were covered over with a mass of leaves. Still shaking, I managed to turn on the front and rear wipers to clean the leaves off. The

Jeep was still running, so I put it in reverse and slowly backed up in an attempt to get back on the main road. When I turned the truck around and surveyed my surroundings, the neighborhood looked like a war zone. Cars were turned upside down, and the streets were littered with fallen trees and large pieces of debris. Live electrical wires snapped by the force of the wind were left hanging down all around like venomous snakes in a jungle, waiting to strike unsuspecting passers by. Through my tears, I could see drivers on their cell phones trying to call for help, but strangely enough, my Jeep was the only vehicle moving on the street, and the only person I had called was Jesus Christ.

I made a three-point turn, being careful of the hanging wires, at least the ones I could see, and then driving over some large tree limb, I proceeded back to the Interstate, totally shaken. As a matter of fact I think I cried the entire 28-mile trip home. Every little gust of wind along the way was a chilling reminder of my horrifying ordeal.

As I traveled along, the question that was in my mind was why did the Lord send me in that direction? Once I was back onto the Interstate, I could see that it was a good thing that I had not gone that way. The "Beltway" (as that part of the Interstate is called) in the College Park area through which the tornado had evidently tracked was littered with hoods of cars, roofing, siding, tree limbs, and I even saw a jack knifed tractor trailer truck through my tears.

Emergency response teams were speeding down the road in their vehicles in the direction of where I had been. I thanked the Lord sincerely for his goodness and mercy in sparing my life, but it was all that I could do to keep my composure to drive home safely.

When I arrived home, I saw the American flag over my door, blowing violently in the wind, and I knew I wanted to take it down to keep it from being lost. When I got out of the Jeep, I looked at the driver's side of my vehicle and it looked like a tree hedge. It was covered with leaves that had been imbedded into the paint of the car from the force of the wind.

I grabbed a ladder out of the garage and went around to my front door. As I walked toward my door, I noticed a woman who I had never seen before standing across the street from my house. She saw me start to climb up the ladder, and she yelled out in a noticeable southern drawl, "Hey gal, you better be careful. Ye're gonna kill yerself doin that." She walked across the street and up the driveway, and then she held the ladder for me. I was grateful for the strange woman's help and I thanked her, though I wondered why she was in our community. It turned out that she was in the neighborhood because she was selling some cleaning products. She could sense my distrust, so she quickly qualified herself by telling me that she had just left the County Police officer's house that was adjacent to mine, as his wife wanted to purchase her products. She also produced some personal checks given to her in payment for her product from other residents in the neighborhood to put me at ease. Her partner was supposed to have picked her up, but had apparently been delayed, so that was the reason why she was standing at the corner.

She helped me to put the ladder back into the garage and we continued talking about why she happened to be on the corner. As she walked down the driveway, she noticed the side of the Jeep. Gasping, she asked in her drawl, "What in the world happened to you?" I looked at her for a few seconds, and then I responded to her question with a question. I asked her, "Do you know Jesus?" She said that she did, and I told her what had happened to me some twenty eight miles away. She thanked the Lord with me and gave me her own testimony about the goodness of the Lord when she was in an abusive relationship.

Unfortunately, people lost their lives in that tornado that day and there were millions of dollars in property damage, and clean up. I have told this story to many, but I never told anyone what I am about to tell now.

After a couple of days had gone by following the tornado, I drove back through College Park looking for that dead-end street with the hills on either side that kept my truck from blowing away. The streets were still littered with downed trees and debris, but now electric power, telephone, and cable company trucks lined the route.

I went through the area that I thought I was in, but I could not find the dead-end street. I even went beyond the point in either direction, thinking that I might have been a little disoriented, but there were no dead-end streets along the Route to be found with hills for protection. On the contrary, all the land sloped down. With this mind boggling and steering revelation, I said to God in my heart, "No matter what it is that You want me to do, I'm doing it." "Just ask."

Chapter 2
The Dream

What? Are you calling me to preach, or write, or what?

*a*few weeks had passed since being pulled miraculously out of the throws of a F3-5 Tornado—I mean like the kind they get in Georgia and Kansas. Over that period of time, I had gladly testified of the power of Jesus Christ to all who would hear, and I was truly ready to do God's bidding whenever he called, just like I promised.

As far as dreams go, I was not the biggest believer that dreams had any real meaning outside of stemming from the events of the day. Normally, I do not even have a lot of dreams, at least not the kind I remember. However, following the tornado event I had a most profound dream, to say the least.

Some weeks had passed since my near death experience in the tornado, and I was back in my normal routine at home and at work. Nothing seemed out of the ordinary, but one night I dreamt that I was standing only a few miles down on the same road where the tornado tracked through. I could see that I was standing on a platform or hill, but I was trying to get to the other side of the road. Somehow I knew that Jesus was coming, and I thought that when he came he would be on the opposite side of the road from where I was standing.

Just below me, on another platform I could see three other people. They were my two daughters and a strange woman I did not know. For some reason, we all seemed to know that Jesus was coming. As I was attempting to cross over to the other side of the road to get to where I thought he'd appear, I heard someone say, "It's too late to go over there now. He is already here."

The next thing I knew, I was then positioned down on the same platform surface where the girls were and I could see a man or an angel walking toward us in a long white robe with a gold braided belt wrapped around his waist. The hair on his head and face was golden-reddish brown like a shiny golden coin and it was a curly to wavy texture. As we stood there watching, I saw his hand reach out in our direction, and although my hand was out stretched to him, his hand bypassed mine. My heart sank a little because I really wanted him to take my hand, but then I felt him give my thigh a strong tap, and I heard him say, "It's time."

His voice was very deep like Yule Brenner the actor, but there was no accent, and it was crystal clear like water. He held out his hand to me, grabbed my hand, and pulled me up onto the platform with him. As we walked together, I listened very intently to hear what he would say. He said to me "Tell them the Beatles are their salvation." My mind was racing with thoughts but I dared not ask him what he meant because he was so austere. I would have laughed at this request, but I knew this was no laughing matter. In my mind I thought, "The beetles?" "What?" "Is He calling me to preach?" "Is he calling me to write?"

Then I was awakened. My heart and my head were racing from the thought of this very clear dream. For awhile, before I could get back to sleep, I laid there beside my husband in our dark bedroom illuminated only by glints of light coming through the blinds from the street lights, wondering about the meaning of this dream. "The beetles; the Beatles," I thought. Are we talking about bugs or the song group?

When I was a teenager I was crazy about the pop group called the Beatles. As a matter of fact, my girlfriends and I use to fantasize that we were married to them. John was my husband. Ironically, my real husband and John Lennon were born on the same day or a day apart in October.

I knew all of their songs and there wasn't a religious one in the bunch to my knowledge, or was there? Then I started to think about the words of their music. Suddenly, like a bright light bulb coming on in our dark room, it dawned on me that the words to most of their songs were all about love. "God is love," I thought. "That's it!"

I finally got back to sleep. When my husband and I got up later that morning, I told him about my dream. My husband with the three saint names, Gregory Augustus James, is so aptly named because he is a real saint. As I told him my dream, I believe that he was with me all the way, right up to the word "beetles," then I think I lost him. But, he was very good about indulging me. I told him that initially I had also thought it was more than a little strange, even funny, but then I went on to tell him about my thoughts on the music of the artists the Beatles. After a little while, he began to understand.

He got up out of bed and without saying a word, he went downstairs into the family room. I could hear him going through the CD cabinet. Then he called upstairs to me and asked where the Beatles "One" CD was. I got up to help him look for it. When we finally found the CD, he went over to his prize music center and dropped in the disc. He set the CD player for repeat play and we sat back and listened to the music and the words. As we listened to the lyrics, we talked through the meaning of the words, and we immediately knew from these words, when put in context

with God's love for mankind, that indeed the Beatles could
be someone's salvation.

Chapter 3
"She (He) Loves You"

A farmer walked into an attorney's office wanting to file for a divorce. The attorney asked "May I help you?" The farmer said, "Yea, I want to get one of those dayvorce's.

The attorney said, "Well, do you have any grounds?" The farmer said, "Yea, I got about 140 acres". The attorney said, "No, you don't understand, do you have a case?" The farmer said, "No, I don't have a Case, but I got a John Deere."

The attorney said, "No you don't understand, I mean do you have a grudge?" The farmer said, "Yea I got a grudge, that's where I park my John Deere." The attorney said, "No sir, I mean do you have a suit"

The farmer said, "Yes sir, I got a suit, I wear to the church on Sundays."

The exasperated attorney said, "Well sir, does your wife beat you up or anything?"

The farmer said, "No sir, we both get up about 4:30."

Finally the attorney says, "Okay, let me put it this way, "WHY DO YOU WANT A DIVORCE?"

And the farmer says, "Well, I can never have a meaningful conversation with her."

To the Runaway

This is certainly not the time for division. During these very trying times we need to stick together, and to stand strong and firm as a country, company, church, team, community and/or family unit. I remember hearing that Satan seeks to steal, kill and destroy. What better way of doing that then by convincing you through his black art of deception that you would be better off on your own, or that the grass is greener on the other side, or that you would be better off away from all that you have known and loved. You see, once you are out there, you are free game for him to toy with and to destroy.

Let's face it; no one gets along perfectly everyday and one hundred percent of the time. Whether you are at home, on the job, at school, on a sports team, or even in church — things happen. (Imagine that!). The problem is that we look to the people and places that we love most to somehow be perfect in every way or to at least be the way we want them to be. But face it, that's just not realistic in this world.

When you think about a runaway, what comes to mind? Usually, you think of the wayward child who felt compelled to leave home because the rules of the house were too restricting. You know, it's the old "to hell with all of you" routine and mentality. Inevitably, after leaving all that they have ever known, they soon discover that not only is the grass not greener on the other side, but as a matter of fact, in many cases it is not even grass.

To you the infamous runaway, if you think you were trying to really hurt someone because they hurt you—well, congratulations! You were very successful. Give yourself a big pat on the back because that mother and/or father of yours that you wanted to pay back for hurting your feelings has been crushed beyond belief. Remember those bothersome siblings of yours who were always getting their way and always in your way? They have been reduced to crying themselves to sleep every night worrying about you. Honey, you are on a royal roll. You should feel so proud.

Remember those old acquaintances of yours, i.e., best friends, girl friends, boy friends, schoolmates, teachers, church members? Well, you'll be glad to know that they are all still reeling from the shock of your leaving without saying goodbye, and that they are missing you an awful lot. You meant more to them than you will ever know. But to top it off, you win the double jackpot because guess what? You hurt yourself, the most. Wow, whatever is a winner like you to do?

While you are pondering that question, let me tell you that you are not the only kind of runaway. There are other kinds of runaways like the person who changes churches every time the pastor does something they don't particularly care for or agree with, and the job hopper who can't take the pressure of being a good employee when the rules get too stringent, or there is real work to perform. There is also the wife, husband, or significant other who flees at the slightest hint of discord in their relationship, or any pressure to commit to doing the right thing. I guess I could go on, but I think you get the picture.

Now that all of you know who you are, and all that you have accomplished as runaways, you should now think about "Whose" you are and how you can correct past mistakes. Become a real winner through the guidance of Jesus Christ.

The words to the Beatles song — "She Loves You" suggests that the first thing you need to do is to kick pride square in the rear and run (don't walk) back down the road to the home you left behind. It has been said that pride comes before a fall. It has also been said that love conquers all. Satan wants you to think that you can't go home again and that nobody loves you anymore. He wants you to beef up your pride so that you will stay away or stay angry on principle. However, since you've been convinced that you've lost their love and can never regain their trust, let me tell you that the Beatles were on to something in their song, "She Loves You", and I believe that Jesus Christ wants you to consider the words to that song, in the context of your current situation, as a message to you from your mom or your dad, the church, or your significant other, or places that you have left behind. You think that you have lost their love, but just today, they had you on their minds. And you know, **"With a love like that, you know you should be Glad! Yeah..."**

In the bible, Jesus tells a parable or life lesson about the prodigal son. It's a story about a young man who asked for his inheritance upfront. After his father gave it to him, he set out to live life on his own terms. This guy didn't leave home to find his fame and fortune, because like many of you, he already had a good life. But, he left home to go live a riotous life and to get from under his father's rule. (Hmmm? Sound familiar?) This guy really messed up big time.

It seems that this young man was one of two sons. The oldest son continued to stay at home and to be obedient to his father, while the younger could not stand to live another day under his father's rule, so he left all that he knew behind him. Most runaways don't get this opportunity like this guy to leave with a substantial amount of money. Usually they leave home broke. This parable that Jesus told goes on to say that after the young man got money from his father, he gathered all he had and took his journey into a far country and there he squandered his property in loose living. When he had spent everything, a great famine arose in that country and he became a poor beggar of sorts. He was broke and hungry and was willing to do anything at this point, so he went to work for a hog farmer feeding hogs. He would have gladly eaten the slop that the hogs ate because no one gave him anything to eat.

However, when he came to himself, he thought about the fact that it wasn't so bad at home after all. He said, "How many of my father's hired servants have bread enough and to spare, but I perish here with hunger! I will arise and go to my father, and I will say to him, Father, I have sinned against heaven and before you; I am no longer worthy to be called your son; treat me as one of your hired servants." (That was better than living with and feeding hogs.) So he packed up and went back home.

The story goes on to say that while the young man was some distance away, his father saw him and had compassion, and ran and embraced him and kissed him. And the son being very surprised by his father's reception said, "Father, I have sinned against heaven and before you; I am no longer worthy to be called your son."

But the father told his servants to go quickly and to bring the best robe and to put it on his son, and to put a ring on his hand, and shoes on his feet. He also told his servants to bring the fatted calf and to kill it, and so that they could celebrate with good food and drink, to eat and make merry. The father was so very pleased that his son was back home again, and he said, "for this my son was dead, and is alive again; he was lost, and is found." And they had a huge celebration with family and friends. **"...with a love like that, you know you should be Glad! Yeah! Yeah! Yeah!"**

Chapter 4
"Get Back"

It's called an apple. Want a bite?

Stevie Wonder once wrote a song that talked about a young man wanting to better his social economic circumstance so much so that it drove him to move away from a life he had always known in a small town for a new life in the big city. In the song, the song writer describes the kid catching a bus to New York City from his small country home. When he arrives in New York, he excitedly steps off the bus at the destination depot, and looking around, he is awe struck by the sights, sounds, and smells of the busy city streets and the tall buildings. But, before this young man can get his bags, some dope pusher or "mule" runs up to him and says "hold this" and dumps drug evidence in his hands. Unbeknownst to the kid, the man has just placed a bag of drugs in his hand to get rid of them because the police were chasing him. Before the kid can say, hold what? The man runs off.

Unfortunately the cops saw the man give the kid the drugs and they arrest this kid on the spot for being in possession of drugs. What a pity. The young man had no idea what the package contained that had been given to him, nor the dirty trick that had been played on him. How sad, because now after being in the big city for all of two minutes, this poor unsuspecting kid who was looking for a better life was now going to be sentenced to twenty years-to-life in prison, all for a bus ride and not being ready for the city.

By no means am I putting down the "big city," because I love the hustle and bustle of big cities with all the job opportunities, the fashion shopping, the shows, the media events, the fine restaurants, and the sophistication and diversity of the many people who reside in the city. But needless to say, many of our young people are not spiritually equipped to make the transition from the farm to futures and to be safe.

Being a recent graduate and having the desire to live in the "big city," or even being fed up enough with your current circumstances does not a big city boy or girl make. Let's be realistic. Along with the glamour and fancy (or not so fancy), but fun lifestyle of living in the metropolis comes cleverly disguised predators. These are the hounds of hell, who are seeking to rip you apart, to spit you out, and to take your mortal soul. They have a track record for making boys think they are girls and for getting both the naive and knowledgeable person to think that it's okay to do unnatural, uncomfortable, or illegal things. They make everything seem so nice and so right. How could anything this great be so wrong? Why do you feel so guilty doing it, at first?

These demons of darkness mingle and mix in with the mainstream, so as not to be readily recognized, and if you are not well grounded in your faith, you can be their next victim. Paul, the apostle of Jesus Christ warns that we wrestle not with flesh, but against powers and principalities in high places. (Yes, there are evil angels on earth, too.)

If you are new to the big city or on your way, it is important that you identify a church home, a doctor, and an attorney. The latter is optional. (Smile) After moving to the city and before you leave home each day, be sure that your feet are shod with the preparation of the gospel of peace. If you haven't done all of that then you might as well pack up and go back home, because that is the only way you can guarantee success in the city. Simply follow the instructions of the apostle Paul in the book of Ephesians – "Therefore, put on the full armor of God, so that when the day of evil comes, you will be able to stand your ground, and after you have done everything, to stand. Stand firm with the belt of truth buckled around your waist, with the breast plate of righteousness and be filled with the readiness that comes from the gospel of peace. In addition to all of this, take up the shield of faith, with which you can extinguish the flaming arrows of the evil one. Take the helmet of salvation and the sword of the spirit, which is the word of God. And, pray in the spirit on all occasions, with all kinds of prayers and requests.

Got that? If not, then take the advice that the Beatles gave to Jojo and Loretta in their classic tune "Get Back", and follow suit. **"Get back to where you once belonged…"**

In the Bible, the gospel of Luke tells how after growing up, Jesus had a "big city" or wilderness experience. He was full of the spirit of God after being baptized and he was led by the spirit to go to a wilderness place where he was tempted for forty days by the devil. During that entire period he fasted, and afterward, he was very hungry. (Some people living in the city have that hunger experience, because housing can be expensive and there is little money left to buy food.)

Seizing on this opportunity, the devil said to him, "If you be the Son of God, command this stone that it be made bread." And Jesus answered him saying. "It is written that man shall not live by bread alone, but by every word of God."

And the devil took him up into a high mountain, and showed him all the kingdoms of the world in a moment of time. And the devil told him that he would give him all power and glory, and everything he showed him in the vision because they were his to give to whomever he pleased. All Jesus had to do was the simple task of falling down and worshipping Satan and it was his.

However, the Lord Jesus answered and told Satan to get behind him because it is written that we should worship the Lord God Almighty, and him only should we serve.

If you arrived in the big city with big ideas, shaky faith, and little street smarts or no ability to just say no to Satan when he temps you with the world, it is strongly suggested that you remember the words of Lennon and McCartney and **"Get back to where you once belonged..."**

And get closer to God.

Chapter 5
"Yesterday"

"When peace like a river attendeth my way; when sorrows like sea billows roll… It is well…"

*I*t's your wedding day. This is the happiest day of your life, at least to this point. All the family has gathered in town for your big day. As you prepare to go to the ceremony, the house is filled with laughter and you joke with your mom and dad about the day finally coming to make you an honest woman. You've been playing the field too long.

You sit in front of the mirror and start to apply your make up. Your mother passes by and pauses. As the two of you gaze into the looking glass, you both realize just how much alike you look. She smiles at you and then asks you what you plan on doing with your hair. The phone rings and it's your girlfriend next door. Your mom yells "you do not have time to talk on the phone. Tell her you'll see her later." Then she asks whether or not you have anything that's blue? (You know the old adage about the bride having to have something old, something new, something borrowed, and something blue.)

You tell your mom that you don't have one thing that's blue and that you had actually forgotten all about the blue. She says, "Never mind. I'11 find something. Maybe your grandmother has something that's blue." Then she goes on chatting about how much blue she has at home, many miles away, and as you listen to your dad and mom debate the pros and cons of going out to purchase something, you trail off in deep thought about your future as Mrs. Best-catch.

In the background you can hear your grandmother asking for some help in the kitchen and everyone is laughing about the lopsided cake she baked. With all the chatter, laughter, and noise from the music your dad is playing you can hardly hear the doorbell ring.

You hear your mom ask in an annoyed way, "Now who could that be?" "We need to get going." Then she says to you "Suzy Que, get the door." Frustrated, but happy you run to the door and swing it open.

There, in front of you stands a drably dressed woman. She could not possibly be a part of the wedding party, dressed like that, but before you can ask her what she wants, she asks you if Suzy Que lives here. You reply curiously that you are Suzy Que. Then you look beyond her to see if she is from the florist or even Publisher's Clearinghouse (after all this is your day) but there is no flower truck, and no cameras. (Darn.)

This grim looking and drably dressed woman tells you she is from the health department and then she hands you an envelope and walks away. "Who was that?" mom asks. "Yeah, who was that?" your dad chimes in.

You tell them that you don't know who the woman was and that she only gave you an envelope. "I hope it's not a court summons," your dad says. You assure him that it is not, and you tell them that the woman said she was from the Health Department. In response to that statement you immediately hear a chorus of voices saying, "The Health Department?" Then everyone is speculating on what the Health Department wants with you. "Maybe it's a job?" your grandmother says. Then your mom says, "Well hurry up and open it up so we can know what they want?"

You quickly rip the letter from its plain white wrapper and read it aloud so to satisfy everyone's curiosity. To save time as you start to put on your dress and read at the same time. "It says, Dear Suzy Que: It is important that you contact our office or your personal physician immediately. Our lab results show that your blood tested positive for H. (You feel the blood drain from your face.) You try to read it again. "Your blood test positive for H and your voice gets a little lower, and a little slower. "Your blood test positive for H - I - V. Early treatment..."

The silence throughout the house is deafening. The only sound in the house is that of water boiling out of a pot onto the flames on the stove. Your mother finally gets the sand out of her mouth and sighs, "Oh, my God in heaven." Devastation is an understatement. Is this some kind of sick joke you think? Who? What? Where? Then you try to quickly remember all of your questionable and unquestionable sexual partners of the past and the unprotected sex, amid the warnings.

You feel your father's hand on your shoulder, and you turn to him and hug him for dear life, wishing that this day had never happened. If only it could by yesterday, again. You think to yourself, "Hey Mom, I finally have something blue."

The Beatles wrote a song that reflects the sentiment of this tale of woe. The song entitled, "Yesterday." After all of the trials and tribulations of today there will be many who will say, like the Beatles, **"Yesterday all my troubles seemed so far away, but now it looks as though they are here to stay, Oh, I believe in yesterday"**

Maybe you have been diagnosed with HIV or some other incurable disease, and you don't know what to do about your tomorrows. Let me strongly suggest that you come to Jesus.

In the bible there is story about a man who came to Jesus to ask him to heal his daughter who was very ill. Jesus told the man to go back home and his daughter would be okay. When the man reached home the next day, sure enough his daughter had been healed, just as Jesus had told him she would be. Out of curiosity, he asked one of his servants at what hour his daughter had started to improve, and when he found out the time, he knew that on yesterday, that was the time Jesus told him to return home.

Jesus Christ wants you to know that he is the same, yesterday, today, and tomorrow. In the bible, John 15:6-7 Jesus says "if a man abide not in me, he is cast forth as a branch and is withered and men gather them and cast them into the fire and they are burned. If you abide in me, and my words abide in you, you shall ask what you will and it shall be done to you." Believe this, and you won't have to believe only in yesterday.

Chapter 6
"I'm a Loser"

(Excuse me, but I'm the King!)

*W*e all have been a disappointment to someone we care about at some point in our lives, if only to ourselves. When I was growing up, I really wanted to make a good impression by doing the right thing, but temptation had a way of easing in unnoticed and the next thing you know, I had taken up with the devil unawares and I was completely convinced that the wrong I was doing was okay.

If you grew up during the 1950s or 60s' or you are a fan of "Nick at Nite" you know about Western/Cowboy TV Shows. (For those of you who are not familiar with

Westerns, reruns are shown everyday on cable television.) Do you remember the old TV Western, Gun Smoke with Mat Dillon who was the Marshal of Dodge City? (It was sort of like a real life Deputy Dog the cartoon. You do know who Deputy Dog is, don't you?)

Anyway, Marshall Dillon was a good guy and all the bad guys feared him. They were always getting the heck out of Dodge to escape him. The funny thing about Satan is that he always gets the heck out of Dodge, so to speak, whenever he sees the sheriff or lynch mob coming just like the bad guys use to do on that show. You see, after tempting you to do wrong, Satan will leave you to take all the weight for your sin. However, when it's time for you to stand before the judge, Satan will return and he will be your number one accuser and witness to the crime. He will even give the "National Enquirer" or "Publication X" an interview, or he will really rub salt into your womb by writing a tell all book about your escapades. Satan just loves to spread the news and to gossip to all who are willing to hear bad tidings of doom and gloom. He also does a little "word-smithing" or just out-and-out lies to make everything sound worse and really juicy. Juice sells.

Usually, when you think about a loser, you think about a person who is not too bright; sort of an outcast from society; a deadbeat, a real bum; or you might even think about a defeated athlete or some other defeated competitor. On the contrary, history records the losing escapades of lots of men and women of high degree, and who were and in many cases still are very successful, but you would think at that point they'd get a clue.

A Loser can be someone who cheats on their spouse, or someone who betrays the trust of a best friend or colleague. A Loser can also be a role model who disappoints those who look up to them. Yes, Losers come in all sizes, shapes, and colors, and they all have the same modus operandi (M.O.). They selfishly do what they want without thought for others. Without fail, Losers always fall from grace after being tempted to do wrong, and then they learn the hard way the real reason for the ten commandments of God. Think it can't happen to you? Think again.

King Solomon was the wisest man to ever live. He was the son of King David; God's elect. Through his wisdom he was able to win battles, settle disputes, make financial gains, write proverbs for living, build the temple of God, and promote the one and only true God to the world, even to the Queen of the South.

But wouldn't you know it, this man who had been divinely granted wisdom and knowledge by God Almighty, became (as old folks use to say) too big for his britches. He went against the will of God and married idol worshiping women of neighboring countries to cut a business deal, and to keep the peace. (Politics makes for strange bedfellows.)

To make matters worse, he started worshiping their manmade idol gods (you know the standard half-man, half-dog, cat, rat, cow, elephant, etc., made out of stone or wood.) and then after hurting God with his actions, he expected everything to be the same. Can you believe that this was the wisest man in the world?

What Solomon forgot was the first commandment which says that God is a jealous god and that we are to have no other gods before Him. (In today's society having other gods might equate to believing in some deity that can't be traced back through prophecies of God with historical facts and archeological codification; or the love of money, power, position, sex, possessions, and the standard half man/half dog, cat, cow, chicken, etc., made out of wood or stone.)

Solomon really blew it. He had it all, but through arrogance and betrayal he earned the title of "Loser". At the top of his game, he stepped over the line and turned a blind eye to the one he should never have crossed, God. When he realized that he had lost God's favor, he wisely repented of his sins, appealing to God's grace and mercy.

Today, we hear about the breakup of marriages and business partnerships. We see televised internationally and through print media blow by blow accounts of great men and women at the top of their games who fall from grace, because they have crossed over the line of no return. These are not notoriously bad people. Without a doubt, some of these individuals know and love God; they regret deeply what they have done; and like Solomon they wisely appeal to God's grace and mercy for forgiveness.

Many of these individuals, both great and small having repented of their sins, no doubt have been forgiven.

The bible tells us that "Jesus Christ gave himself for our sins, that he might deliver us from this present and evil world, according to the will of God and our Father, to whom be glory for ever and ever, Amen." Therefore these individuals are no longer losers but winners once again through Christ.

In case you have been at the top of your game, in a good relationship, or position, but now you are on your way down, because you crossed over the line, think about the words of John Lennon of the Beatles when he sings, "I'm a loser, and I'm not what I appear to be." Could this be you?

If you are a Loser and you don't know where to start, let me suggest that you pray as David prayed in Psalms 51: 10-12. "Create in me a clean heart, O God; and renew a right spirit within me. Cast me not away from thy presence and take not thy Holy Spirit from me. Restore to me the joy of thy salvation and uphold me with thy free spirit," because, **"I'm a loser..."**

Chapter 7
"Help!"

*W*hat does it mean when somebody says they have "come full-circle"? To most of us it means that we have made it. In business we shoot for the moon and proudly proclaim the news to all when we "have arrived". Headlines like "John Smith takes the helm at XYZ Company," "Joe Blow wins another tournament tour de force," or "Mary Contrary is the first woman to ever..." illuminate internet screens and the pages of the local newspapers and magazines everyday. But what does life dictate that coming full circle really mean?

It means we start out as helpless babes in arms, we mature, we grow older, and ultimately we end up as helpless old babes in arms. That's life, and we all have to go that route if we should live so long.

Baby Boomers will soon be the largest living elderly population the world has known for many, many centuries, if not ever. We raised our children to be strong and independent, to achieve and to go out and get `em. But, we did not teach them to come back to the farm or family business to help out. We also misled them in their understanding of independence. They think it's a synonym for not being there. While we were showing our children the ropes of being successful in today's society, we neglected to let them know that what goes around, comes around, full circle.

Whatever happened to families living in one home (or at least in the same community) with everyone pitching in to help one another? What ever happened to families like the Walton's or (God help us) even the Ewing's? In today's society, two people live alone in a 3500 square foot dwelling, and mom and dad live in a nursing home hundreds of miles away, feeling useless and waiting to die. I believe that Jesus Christ would cry foul to that. Through his exemplary life and teachings, Jesus shows us that he wants the family unit together in prayer and support of one another, pooling spiritual and financial resources, so that each person lives a full, quality of life, while feigning off the wilds of the devil. And, you don't have to limit your help to just family members.

My husband and I befriended an old woman when we were quite young. She was in her late 80's and we were in our late 20's. She was a member of our church at the time, and we sat on the same pew. She and I were also members of the same church ladies organization. It started off with our offering her transportation home. We found her to be very intelligent, interesting, entertaining, and knowledgeable. She loved to travel and had traveled the world over on her own. One of the only places in the world that she had not visited was Australia, and she and I were to plan a trip to go there. She had accomplished so very much as a black woman growing up in an era following slavery. She wasn't a slave, but her grandparents were. Our friend owned prime property in Washington, DC and in Virginia. As a young woman she even owned one of the first model T Fords. She retired from the government, and she was highly respected as the matriarch of a very old and large Virginia family. She new the value of a dollar and she and her late husband had established themselves very well financially.

Our relationship grew from rides home to rides to and from church. She and I would go on outings together to the shopping center, to the theater to see plays, to club meetings, to luncheons, or to dinner. My husband would mow her lawn and do little repairs around her house, and the next thing you knew, we were just like family in everyway. She never had any children of her own, but she did have a lot of nieces and nephews. We grew to love her like a mother or grandmother and she loved us. I knew as much about her finances as any niece, nephew, or her attorney. Our relationship flourished for several years. Over that time we could sense and see the envy of her relatives at her attentiveness and love for us.

When she was about 98 years old, the bones and muscles in her legs were so weakened that she had difficulty walking with her fancy cane. Whenever we walked together, she would hold on to my husband's or my arm. One day, I suggested to her that she trade in her fancy cane for a walker, because I feared she might eventually fall and seriously injure herself. She got a walker and she started taking physical therapy for her legs, but it was too little, and too late. From that point on, I would go over on Sunday mornings to dress her for church. She had a niece who lived nearby who cared for her during the week, and a roomer who lived in the upstairs apartment in her three story townhouse, that was just minutes from the Capitol, but nonetheless, she wanted me to dress her on Sunday. We had become the very best of friends. We talked at least once a day and we would plan what we were going to wear to different events. My children and our parents grew to love her, too. She was a real jewel.

It was nothing for her to travel out of town. So, when she went to her home in Virginia one Thanksgiving, we did not think much about it, until we got a call from one of her nieces telling us that she had been hospitalized for a possible stroke. Hearing the news, we were both saddened.

We called the hospital to inquire about her health, and we were told that she was improving. We immediately made plans to go to Virginia that weekend. When we arrived, she was very happy to see us. She kept telling us that she just wanted to come back home to Washington. The problem was that she could no longer walk. She did not have a stroke, but her leg bones and muscles were too weak to sustain her, and that is why she collapsed. This very competent, independent, well spoken, dignified, but no longer spry woman only wanted someone to help her to continue to live her life at home, as she wanted to.

Unfortunately, as close as we were to her, we were not family, and our hands were tied. Her family members put her into a nursing home, against her wishes. Since she could no longer walk, she wanted to identify a daily caregiver in the family, if possible, so that she could live at home. Of no fewer than ten nieces and nephews, to whom she had generously dispersed money from one of her savings accounts (as Christmas gifts just a year earlier, so that they would not have to pay inheritance tax), not one of them would volunteer to assist her in living in her home, nor would any of their children. She had to nearly spend the rest of her life's savings and her government pension, paying well over $2500 per month for care in a nursing home. (*I don't know. There may have been circumstances that came into play that might have prevented any of them from helping their dear aunt.*)

We visited our friend as often as we could, but she was unhappy and she seemed to be deteriorating fast. Maybe she was just getting older. On one occasion when we visited, she complained that she did not have any real family (children). On our last visit, following her 105th birthday, she was a little peeved with us for not coming to see her for a while. By that time, she seemed to have accepted what she could not change and was for the most part content. We lost our friend that winter. It was a sad day, indeed.

At her funeral, the preacher told the mourners that when our friend joined church, she filled out a membership card and that she listed as her favorite hymn the song, "If I can Help Somebody." ("...Then my living shall not be in vain.")

Jesus wants Generation X to pass along to Generation Y the words of the following Beatles' song to consider in this life, so that your living will not be in vain:

"...Help me if you can, I'm feeling down... Won't you please, please help me?"

In Mark 7:6-13, Jesus said, "Isaiah was right when he prophesied about you hypocrites; as it is written: These people honor me with their lips, but their hearts are far from me. They worship me in vain; their teachings are but rules taught by men. You have let go of the commands of God and are holding on to the traditions of men. You have a fine way of sitting aside the commands of God in order to observe your own traditions. For Moses said honor your father and mother and anyone who curses his father or mother must be put to death. But you say that if a man says to his father or mother whatever help you might otherwise have received from me is Corban (that is a gift devoted to God), then you no longer let him do anything for his father or mother. Thus you nullify the word of God by your traditions that you have handed down. And you do many things like that."

Jesus Christ wants you to know the word of God and to **help** your parents and the elderly. Listen to their pleas for help, and come full circle in the Kingdom of God.

Chapter 8
"Hey Jude"

Someone reading this book has been through the emotional trauma of having your best friend(s) who you entrusted to betray you. Someone else may have been misjudged and as a result you lost a job, a business deal, or a legal case, and the only thing you are guilty of is doing what you know is right. Now, let's take this to a higher level. You are married and you caught your cheating heart spouse or significant other in a compromising situation. What about murder or children dying senseless deaths? Despite your hurt, suffering, and pain, is your heart big enough to allow you to continue to love unconditionally, and to forgive those who hurt you so deeply?

I'm sure the standard response goes something like this: "Wait a minute." "Timeout." "Fat chance." "This ain't happening." "She/he left me, betrayed me, cheated on me, physically assaulted me, lied on me, ran away, stole my, took the life of my…, fired me, and you want me to take this to a higher level and to do what?" "I'm the one who's been hurt. I'm the one on the losing end." "I think not. I am much too cool for that, and besides what will my forgiving them and loving someone like that accomplish?"

Good question! Actually, it will accomplish volumes. Not only will it improve your health and prevent serious diseases like cancer, when we forgive others and when we do well toward those who have wronged us in anyway, we are considered to be the children of the most High God. As such, we are highly favored and blessed. According to God's word, we also heap burning coals on the heads of our enemies. We set ourselves up in a leadership roll extraordinaire, and God shows his approval by showering us with blessings before our enemies.

In many cases, following an angry mix up, deep in your heart, you know you want things to be good like they were before. Married couples know this all to well. It's like how you feel after a bad argument. You feel really hurt and betrayed, but, you also know how nice it feels to make up. I believe it's even better to forgive and to forget when it's for something of great magnitude, because when you forgive without thought for your own feelings, the recipient of your graciousness is forever in your debt. Think about it.

To be on the receiving end of physical or emotional pain is a terrible thing. Take for example the life of Jesus Christ, and how he suffered humiliation and the physical pain of being whipped and nailed to a cross for our sins. You should know that he empathizes with you in hurtful situations. However, as an example to us for living, Jesus asked God to forgive those who were cruelly inflicting pain on him.

When you have been unjustly wronged and are experiencing the resulting emotional or physical pain, you have two choices. You can make it worse or you can make it better. Paul McCartney gives the perfect advice in his song "Hey Jude." "**...Remember to let her into your heart, and then you can start to make it better...**"

There was a great apostle of Jesus Christ (though he was not one of the original twelve) whose name was Paul. Paul wrote a letter to the Romans and it is recorded in the New Testament of the Bible. In the 12th Chapter of his letter to the Romans, Paul gives perfect advice for getting along with your fellow man. He says to let love be without dissimulation. Abhor that which is evil and cleave to that which is good. (In other words, don't make it bad, take a sad song and make it better.) He goes on to say that we should be kind and affectionate to one another with brotherly love, in honor, preferring one another; and not to be slothful in business, but fervent in spirit; serving the Lord."

He also tells us to bless those who persecute us. Bless and curse not. (Take a deep breath, let it out and let it in. Don't walk around with a chip on your shoulder.) God said, avenge not yourselves, but rather give place to wrath; for it is written, "Vengeance is mine, I will repay," says the Lord. **"...then you'll begin to make it better, better, better..."**

Chapter 9
"Act Naturally"

*H*ollywood is the place where dreams come true, or so they say. Can't you hear that music in the air? They are playing your song. Listen. "Overture; hit the lights; this is it; we'll hit the heights; and oh what heights we'll hit. On with the show this is it!"

Yes, dreams do come true in Hollywood. Many young, talented, and ambitious individuals convinced of their thespian skills have deplaned in Los Angeles, California looking for their pot of gold at the rainbow's end at Hollywood and Vine. Many of them have actually made a movie or two. (Crowd scenes don't count.) But, for many others the closest they ever got to working in the movies was when they delivered lunch to the studio. Only a small fraction of the thousands who come to Hollywood to act can say that they've really made it.

This is so sad for the many, but true. You can count on your fingers and toes the top actors for any period in time. But what makes these individuals different from all of the rest? Could it be God's divine will and blessings? What about hair or eye color? Maybe it's their perfect height or weight? How about just being in the right place at the right time? Line memory? Chemistry? Sacrifice? We could go on and on, but what do these successful few have that others don't have?

The answer is perhaps yes to all of the above. Making it big in TV, the movies, and in the music industry is like playing the slot machine in Vegas. Sometimes you hit; sometimes you don't hit at all; and then sometimes you hit really big. But, you can count on your fingers and toes the number of people who really hit big playing the slots for any period of time, just like top actors in Hollywood.

It's a real gamble, but what happens to the individuals who really make it big in acting, music, or even sports? Well obviously their lives are changed beyond belief. The house (mansion) that the average celebrity lives in is not just a big spacious house; in some cases it's a small city. (Have you ever seen the television show called "Cribs"?

Oh, and the car, I mean cars. They are unmistakably the very best that money can buy. No silly, they don't drive them—at least not everyday like you and I. They keep them in a garage and they hire limousines or drive sport utility vans to get around town. Jewels, stocks, bonds, furs, and business investments are what their accountants tell them they need to keep the money fluid. But, this lifestyle of fabulous lavishness comes with a hefty price tag. It's called "Acting Naturally."

Oh, did I forget to tell you about the abundance of fear that the rich and famous have for their lives, and as a result many have to live under heavy jail like security to keep the fans, robbers, paparazzi, and everyday run of the mill nut cases away? And, you must know about the tasty dust they have to lick off the boots of producers and directors just to keep the paychecks coming. As if that were not enough, they are physically, mentally and spiritually beat down with long grueling hours of filming, starvation diets, and publicity spots. This darker side of the good life also comes with a hefty price tag, and it's also called Acting Naturally.

There must be a better way, you say? You are right. God wants us to have the good life and to have it more abundantly through Him. The apostle Paul wrote that we should always rejoice in the Lord and to let our moderation be known to all men. He also wrote that our Lord and Savior Jesus Christ is with us all the time and all we need to do is pray to him in sincerity and thankfulness and he will regard our prayers. Paul says that we should not worry about anything but to keep our hearts and minds on Jesus to experience unbelievable peace. And finally, he writes that we should keep our minds on whatever is true, honest, just, pure, lovely, of good report, virtuous, and praiseworthy.

God wants those he has blessed with blossoming careers in music, stage, TV, or motion pictures to use their money making popularity and acting clout to say no to rolls that celebrate Satan with unnatural sex, vulgarities, needless violence, and glorifying crime and witchcraft. Celebrities, you have been blessed by the best, so do not dismiss your values and lower your standards to do any movies, television shows, or sing songs that pollute young minds and otherwise negatively affect society. Movie and television actors should be selective in the rolls they accept as well as in their lifestyles.

I remember renting a video once, that I knew would be hilarious, because of the actors who were playing in it. Before I could get half way through the movie, I had to turn it off because every other word was profane.

This vulgarity did not add anything to the comedy of the movie. In fact, it took away. If there had been less profanity, I probably would have been rolling in the aisles with laughter. I would surely have shared it with family and guests.

Years ago, I heard a lady say about a very popular comedian back in the 70's, that he would be really funny if he didn't "cuss" so much. I really understand what she meant by that, now.

Because media and music stars are so powerful in today's society, they should use their star influence for the betterment of mankind. They should also use their financial resources to help others, not just in their industry, but they should reach out and reach back to the struggling neighborhood, school system, and churches from which they came and put some of that box office money back into the community and not in a garaged car. There is nothing wrong with liking and having nice things, but excess in anything is a sin.

This is such a small price to pay for the real "good life" here and in the hereafter. It's nothing like what the average actor pays today or the price tag that Beatles describe in their song, "Act Naturally."

"They're going to put me in the movies. They're gonna make a big star out of me."...

To any movie star, wrap artist, media celebrity, or "wanna be" who says that's hogwash, remember this: You've been blessed with the power. Use it wisely, or you will be

"The biggest fool that ever hit the big time." And all you've got to do is "act naturally."

Chapter 10
"Eleanor Rigby"

There but by the grace of God, go I.

*H*urrying here and there along city sidewalks, one cannot help but notice the large numbers of homeless people that seem to have surfaced in recent years. When I was young, a "homeless person" was referred to as a tramp, hobo, or vagrant. These individuals didn't let any grass grow under their feet. They moved around from town to town on the nation's rails, stowed away in freight cars of trains. They would find employment wherever they could for a meal or wage, and at the end if the day their bed of choice was a park bench. When freight trains came through a town they would reduce their speed as they went across traffic crossings, and slow just enough so that the hobo was able to board unnoticed into one of the open freight cars and move on. Usually, it was the town police who ran these roving rogues out of town on a rail.

Times have changed, and today homelessness comes in all sizes, shapes, ages and colors. Homeless people are everywhere, but where do they all come from?

I researched this phenomenon and found that there are two significant reasons why we see so many homeless people today — they are (1) a growing shortage of affordable rental housing and (2) a simultaneous increase in poverty. The National Commission on Homelessness says, "Homelessness and poverty are inextricably linked." Low-income people are often unable to pay for food, shelter, daycare, and healthcare, and when faced with making choices, many times the home is the first to go.

The normal response of most people to this fact is that it's a shame, and it is. But what's worse is that it can happen to anybody. If you or I lose our jobs today or tomorrow, or we come down with a serious illness or have a serious accident, we too may be only one paycheck away from living on the streets.

The lack of affordable housing and poverty are not the only factors that have contributed to the rise in homelessness. Consider the battered woman, the mentally ill patient no longer housed by state supported mental health care facilities, and welfare reform which has successfully reduced caseloads, but has left a host of people who are not receiving benefits and who are not gainfully employed or employable. Fewer to no job opportunities, falling incomes, and less secure jobs all contribute to the increasing poverty we are witnessing today in the world's most powerful and richest nation. It takes more than minimum wage to pay the rent for a one or two-bedroom house or apartment in today's economy.

Jesus Christ wants us to remember the poor. The Beatles did in their song entitled Eleanor Rigby. This song seems to be about a poor woman living in a church shelter. She gathers rice off the church floor after a wedding, maybe for food, like Ruth who gleaned the fields of Boaz of the House of David. Perhaps she's a lonely bag lady, as this woman keeps all she has in a jar. She lives and dies in the church and no one remembers her and no one is saved as a result of caring for her. Think about the words to this familiar Beatles tune and consider the blight of the homeless.

"Ah, look at all the lonely (homeless) **people; where do they all come from..."**

The Lord makes the poor and the rich. He raises the poor out of the dust, and lifts the beggar up from the dunghill, to set them among princes, and to make them inherit the throne of glory. For the pillars of the earth are the Lord's and he has set the world upon them. I Samuel 2:7-8

Please, remember the poor. But by the grace of God there goes you or I. **"...All the lonely people. Where do they all belong?"**

By the way, they next time you see one of those guys with a sign that reads "help me get a sandwich" or "I'm hungry", why don't you surprise them with a twenty dollar bill instead of the same small change or nothing at all.

Chapter 11
"Nowhere Man"

*I*t is absolutely beautiful to see the joint worship of our Father God by a mixture of races in the same church. It looks like heaven on earth.

I grew up in a segregated society in the south, and church was no exception. I was taught that there were lines you just did not cross, and I wasn't trying to cross any. I was perfectly satisfied in my world that my parents had forged out for me out of hard work and their love for me and for God.

I guess a lot of people thought that way. As a matter of fact, many actually thought that the bible condoned separation of groups of people. After all, the bible clearly tells how the Jews were separate from the Gentiles and how these descendants of Abraham were told not to mingle or marry outside of their faith (not race).

But why was this so? They were told to do so because God knew if these people (many who were weak minded in the faith like many of us) were to mingle and mix outside of their faith (not race) it would tend to weaken them and they would begin to do things outside of His law.

In the book of Judges in the old testament of the bible there is a story about a very famous Judge and man of God named Samson. Samson had been made exceptionally strong by God. In the 16th chapter of the book of Judges it tells about how this exceptionally strong man and avenger of his people fell in love with a woman name Delilah who was not of his faith, and of how she continuously troubled him to tell her the secret of his strength. She was doing this because she had been promised riches by the Philistines if she could find out and tell them how they could destroy Samson.

Time and time again Delilah tried and failed, but finally Samson in a moment of passion, told her all. She quickly used his secret against him and he became powerless. The Philistines captured him and put out his eyes. Then they tied him to a mill grinder where in his powerlessness he was made to walk in circles all day. God had left Samson because of his failure to be faithful.

If you are not strongly committed in your faith in God, your non-committed friend or spouse through their lifestyle and beliefs could cause you to fall from the strict teachings, thus weakening your faith. It's like mixing religion with the secular. (Reference Galatians 1:6-8) On the contrary, if you are strongly committed, you can have power and influence over others to change them.

In the word of God, we learn how Jesus Christ through his death on the cross, took on the sins of the entire world, not just one segment of society. Through his resurrection he became the doorway to eternal life to the one and only true God for any and all who would believe and have a strong faith in that fact regardless of their former beliefs or disbeliefs.

So, how is it possible for a, God fearing, society to become one of segregationists or separatists? That's simple. The answer is Satan. Satan wants to put out the eyes of all of God's people. Just like the Philistines did to Samson. He wants to blind them to the truth of their strength, take away their God fearing point of view, and then lead them down a circular path that goes *nowhere* like the mill grind, while whispering sweet nothings in their ears their entire life's journey, and telling them that they are either superior or inferior to others. This is a ploy to make them miss their earthly blessings and a sure ticket for them to accompany Satan to eternal damnation.

Paul McCartney and John Lennon pinned the words to the song "Nowhere Man," and Jesus Christ wants you to consider whether or not you want to go through life blinded and void of understanding or to enjoy the richness and blessings of living in peace in a diverse society.

"Doesn't have a point of view. Knows not where he's going to. Isn't he a bit like you and me?"

Jesus Christ does not want you to miss out on all that God desires to bless you with because you choose wrongly to be a *Nowhere Man.*

John 4:6-10, tells of a Samaritan woman who came to draw water from Jacob's well, and when she was near enough, Jesus said to her, "Will you give me a drink?" The Samaritan woman said to him, "you are a Jew and I am a Samaritan woman. How can you ask me for a drink?" (Jews did not associate with Samaritans.) But, Jesus answered her and said, "If you knew the gift of God and who it is that asks you for a drink, you would have asked him and he would have given you living water."

The apostle Paul says in Ephesians 2:11-19 that we are one in Christ. "Therefore, remember — formerly you who are gentiles by birth and called "uncircumcised" by those who call themselves "the circumcision" (that done in the body by the hands of men)—remember that at that time you were separate from Christ, excluded from citizenship in Israel and foreigners to the covenants of the promise, without hope and without God in the world. But now in Christ Jesus you are no longer foreigners and aliens, but fellow citizens with God's people and members of God's household, built on the foundation of the apostles and prophets, with Christ Jesus himself as the chief cornerstone. In him the whole building is joined together and rises to become a holy temple in the Lord..."

"...This mystery is that through the gospel the Gentiles are heirs together with Israel, members together of one body, and share together in the promise in Christ Jesus." That means that you do not have to be a nowhere man, in a nowhere land, making nowhere plans for nobody.

Chapter 12
"Ticket to Ride"

A First Class Ticket to Heaven or Hell

*B*ack in the 60's and probably before, free love, smoking Pot (marijuana) and "doing your own thing" became the theme of the age for many. "Make love, not war" was the chant of the young masses, and the question of the era was, why get married when you can simply shack up?"

Satan got a ringside seat for this one, because he knew it was going to go the distance. Morality was for squares. There was a new in-crowd, with a new way of walking and a new way of talking in town. There was even a hit song about it. "I want sexual healing."

Young men were deceptively happier than they had ever imagined, since it was no longer like pulling teeth to convince some young girl to have sex, I mean to make love. And, in case you did hit upon a hard-nose, diehard virgin, all you had to do was to get her tipsy and you were half way there. Today, that might be date rape pills in a drink.

Young women on the other hand were also deceptively happier than they had ever imagined, as they found a replacement for being born beautiful or being on the cheer leading squad to get the attention of the boy of their dreams. All they had to do was to demonstrate loose or low morals and a willing spirit, and Bingo! — he was telling her what she wanted to hear; at least for the moment. No matter how brief the moment might have been.

Oh, didn't I tell you earlier that Satan knew this trend would go the distance? Well, it did and it has. We are now in the 21st Century and it is still going strong. I must admit, with every succeeding round in the fight ring of life, things are getting bloody and the opponent is really nasty.

Young ladies are no longer referred to as babes but bit#*es. In today's world, they not only have to get naked in front of the object of their affection, but now they have to strip down and bear all to the world to compete for attention. The number of cases of venereal diseases has quadrupled. New and incurable diseases have come into existence, like herpes (the "Scarlet Letter") and AIDs (the "Black Plague").

From all of this you might have expected a real population boom, and it did increase a little with all of the births out of wedlock, but we also experienced the highest rate of infant mortality since keeping record with the lack of pre-natal care by unprepared young girls who did not have a clue about being mothers, or for caring for their unborn babies and ABORTION.

Live babies sucked out of existence, just like a piece of worthless lent on a floor being sucked up by a vacuum and later dumped and forgotten; for who remembers lent.

Satan is jumping up and down for joy in his front row, ring side seat. His deceptive evil has got mankind on the ropes and they are being beat to death. Remember the Rocky movie. It's pitiful. But, Jesus Christ is our coach and he speaks to us through various means. He has chosen to speak to the young women of today, because he has chosen them to be of great influence in the body of Christ. Wherever they go the good men will follow. The women of today are offered a free ticket to paradise, and they would be foolish to turn it in.

Young women everywhere are choosing morality over licentiousness. They are choosing to have their babies instead of aborting them, and they are choosing to wait for Mr. Right (remember him?) before jumping into bed with every Tom, Dick, or Harry. They are choosing marriage over shacking up, and family life over loving the one you're with. They are choosing to be called by their Christian names, and not female dogs. (Of all of great beasts God created, what idiot thought it was flattering to call himself a dog?)

Satan is getting really nervous now, because he has put in an extra bet that seems to be slipping away right in front of his eyes. He can't believe that his deceptive coaching is failing and he is mad. This new way of thinking by women reminds you of the song "Ticket to Ride" by the Beatles.

Young lady, have you got your first class ticket? If so, then climb aboard to the good life.

Chapter 13
"Every Little Thing"

*M*any men for most of their lives, from puberty to manhood, think of themselves as "players" or "playboys." They are the mighty hunters, and their conquests are a testament to their reputations. See them as they cruise down the street, sometimes alone and sometimes with the pack (crew, gang, fellas) ever watchful. Their heads turn 360 degrees as they zero in on the catch of the day. These hot guys range in style from the smooth, the suave, and the sophisticated to the cool, the slick, and the quick. They come in all sizes, shapes and colors, and the hook-up line they use to get the girl is generally always the same. (Duh!)

Now there is nothing wrong with that. After all, it takes a lot for a guy to get up the nerve to be possibly rejected, and if they are rejected, then they at least need sufficient cool to retreat and regroup to hunt another day.

But even the "Player" or "Playboy" meets the woman if his dreams one day and from that moment on, he is a new creature. "One enchanted evening, you may see a stranger across a crowded room, and you'll know even then, that you will see her again and again." Yes it's your wife to be. It's your other half. "Adam" or "Player", this is the woman who has your missing rib.

She's not a model, but she's beautiful. She's not razor thin, but she is finely minted. She is not the bell of the ball, but she is ringing your chimes. Look at her. Now imagine a life with her forever. See that smile. It's gorgeous. One might say even addictive. What wouldn't you do to make her all yours? You are completely smitten.

Oh, don't worry about any rejection here. Trust me, it's mutual. You may have to help her get rid of some baggage, but it'll be worth it. Go on and pop the question, man. Even if you meet a little turbulence along the way, you'll get through it as you think about "every little thing."

Grow old together and savor her charm and grace. Caress her body only and always think of every little thing she does. The Beatles song, "Every Little Thing," says this well.

"Every little thing she does, she does for me..."

Jesus Christ wants husbands to love their wives, just as He loves the Church and gave himself up for her to make her holy, cleansing her by the washing with water through the word, and to present her to himself as a radiant church, without stain, or wrinkle or any other blemish, but holy and blameless. The apostle Paul says, "In the same way, husbands ought to love their wives as their own bodies. He who loves his wife loves himself. After all, no one ever hated his own body, but feeds and cares for it, just as Christ does the church—for we are members of his body. For this reason a man will leave his father and mother and be united to his wife, and the two will become one flesh." (Ephesians 5:25-32)

For those guys who would marry, God already has the perfect mate for you, and you should remember, **"Every little thing; every little thing… she does for you."**

Chapter 14
"Devil in Her Heart"

*I*t's been a few years since you said those magic words, "I do." The kids and the bills have increased over time. You and your wife's weight has also increased, but at least she's trying to take it off. Now you are no slim Jim. You've been pumping aluminum cans and filling out your easy chair. Can you believe that you're starting to have some doubts about the ole charm, since the wife reads herself to sleep every night or surfs the Internet until you are asleep.

So, you think to yourself it might be fun to do something different. Maybe you should just get out with the boys to break up the monotonous routine. Maybe you should take a few extra trips out of town, to get away from it all. What harm can that be? To answer your question, there is actually no harm at all, unless you get caught up with the devil.

There is this woman on the job; at the club; or at church who is always in your face, and she seems to be so nice. You like her as a friend. She makes you laugh, and you can't help but notice that she has a nice body and she always says the right things. As a matter of fact, if you were still available, you might have to add her to your collection of conquests. After all you were a real "lady killer" in your day, and you still know how to turn on the ole charm. But let's be realistic, you are married; she knows it; and this case is closed. But you find yourself thinking about her more and more. What's a poor guy to do?

George Harrison of the Beatles wrote this advice and Jesus advises you to consider his words.

"She's got the devil in her heart"... No, no, nay will she deceive?"

In the book of Proverbs, King Solomon gives this warning — "My son, pay attention to my wisdom, listen well to my words of insight, that you may maintain discretion and your lips may preserve knowledge. For the lips of an adulteress drip honey, and her speech is smoother than oil; but in the end she is bitter as gall, sharp as a double-edge sword. Her feet go down to death; her steps lead straight to the grave. She gives no thought to the way of life; her paths are crooked, but she knows it not."

"Now then my son, listen to me; do not turn aside from what I say. Keep to a path far from her, do not go near the door of her house, lest you give your best strength to others and your years to one who is cruel; lest strangers feast on your wealth and your toil enrich another man's house." (Divorce and alimony can be sobering.)

"At the end of your life you will groan, when your flesh and body are spent. You will say how you hated discipline! How my heart spurned correction! I would not obey my teachers or listen to my instructors. I have come to the brink of utter ruin in the midst of the whole assembly."

"Drink water from your own cistern, running water from your own well. Should your springs overflow in the streets, your streams of water in the public squares? Let them be yours alone, never to be shared with strangers. (No wife swapping.) May your fountain be blessed, and may you rejoice in the wife of your youth. A loving doe, a graceful deer, may her breast satisfy you always, may you ever be captivated by her love."

"Why be captivated, my son, by an adulteress? Why embrace the bosom of anther man's wife? For a man's ways are in full view of the Lord, and he examines all his paths. The evil deeds of a wicked man ensnare him; the cords of sin hold him fast. He will die for lack of discipline, led astray by his own great folly." (Proverbs 5)

"She's got the devil in her heart. No, she's an angel sent to me." Be wise and never forget that the devil can disguise himself as an angel of light.

Chapter 15
"All You Need Is Love"

*I*t's too bad that Adam and Eve didn't realize that all they needed was love in the Garden of Eden. It's also too bad the children of Israel didn't realize that all they needed was love as they wondered forty years in the desert, and God help us, it's too bad that so many of us don't realize that all we need is love to live happily in this world.

God is love. He created us with that love and he is, as he was, from the beginning, poised and ready to supply our every need because of that love. Sounds a little too simple doesn't it? Maybe we think we need to take a bite of an apple or murmur a lot to see what we can get, after all who knows better then we do what we need. Think again.

Let me tell you a little story about the all knowing, all seeing God of love. One night I was awaken from my sleep and I thought of a major bill that was due the next day that I forgot I had not paid, yet. It was one of those automatic bank deduction payments. Unfortunately, it was mortgage week, not to mention that we had just written a check for $5000.00 to hold some land. We had exhausted most of our savings trying to help our daughter to reestablish herself in her new home. I was sick, because one way or another, something was not going to be honored at the bank. I started to worry, but then I stopped short and said to myself, I am not going to worry, I am just going to pray. I did not ask the Lord for help specifically, at least not right away. Lying in my bed, I started saying the Lord's Prayer. "Our Father, which art in heaven, hallowed be thy name; thy kingdom come; thy will be done in earth as it is in heaven. Give us this day our daily bread, and forgive us our trespasses as we forgive those who trespass against us. And, lead us not into temptation but deliver us from evil. For thine is the kingdom, and the power, and the glory, forever. Amen.

After saying this prayer that I learned as a child, I simply said, Lord, I'm putting this in your hands, because there is nothing that I can do. Please help.

After I prayed I got up for a drink of water. I quenched my thirst with a cool drink from the fridge, and then I wondered into a front bedroom where the window shade was up. I could see the midnight blue sky. It was so clear. There wasn't a cloud in the sky. The moon was a bright white crescent shape and the planet Venus was the brightest star right next to it. As I looked at the sky, it looked just like the Planetarium at the Smithsonian or rather the Planetarium was an exact replica of what I saw that night. Every star was in its place. I thought, wow, the same God who created me, created all of this. The stars are still in the same position where God hung them billions of years ago. But what is truly amazing is that this same great God of creation is mindful of little ole me.

So, I went back to bed with that thought in mind. I didn't know what to do about the bill, but when I thought about how awesome God is, and about all of his creations, miracles, and blessing of love in the universe, I did not feel the need to worry about a thing. I trusted him to help me, because he loves me.

I went back to sleep and never gave the bill a second thought, until the next day. While preparing to go to work, I felt that I should go on-line and check our bank account. To my great surprise, there was a deposit of $6000.00 in our account that I was not expecting for another two weeks. It was made two days earlier that week. God had answered my prayer before I prayed. After turning flips, I thanked him greatly for His love for me.

Hello Bunkie. Feeling tired and blue? Everything is about you? Can't seem to have a good time anymore? Forgot the words to Lionel Ritchie's song "Jesus Is Love"? (Remember, "He won't let you down.")

Well, cheer up Bunkie. Over your head there may be rain clouds in the air, but there is a God up there and everywhere, too, and He says all you need is love. Ponder the words to John Lennon's song, take two aspirin, and call on Jesus in the morning.

"All you need is love, love; love is all you need..."

God is Love. Think on all of these things.

Printed in the United States
26918LVS00003B/247-378